8-19-2021

HELPING YOURSELF
HELPING OTHERS

# Dealing with
# TEEN
# PREGNANCY

Kristin Thiel

Cavendish
Square

New York

Published in 2020 by Cavendish Square Publishing, LLC
243 5th Avenue, Suite 136, New York, NY 10016

Library of Congress Cataloging-in-Publication Data

Names: Thiel, Kristin, 1977- author.
Title: Dealing with teen pregnancy / Kristin Thiel.
Description: New York : Cavendish Square, [2020] | Series: Helping yourself, helping others | Audience: Grades 7-12. | Includes bibliographical references and index.
Identifiers: LCCN 2018058463 (print) | LCCN 2018060633 (ebook) | ISBN 9781502646378 (ebook) | ISBN 9781502646361 (library bound) | ISBN 9781502646354 (pbk.)
Subjects: LCSH: Teenage pregnancy--Juvenile literature. | Sex instruction for teenagers--Juvenile literature.
Classification: LCC HQ759.4 (ebook) | LCC HQ759.4 .T485 2020 (print) | DDC 613.9071/2--dc23
LC record available at https://lccn.loc.gov/2018058463

Editorial Director: David McNamara
Editor: Caitlyn Miller
Copy Editor: Rebecca Rohan
Associate Art Director: Alan Sliwinski
Designer: Ginny Kemmerer
Production Coordinator: Karol Szymczuk
Photo Research: J8 Media

The photographs in this book are used by permission and through the courtesy of: Cover wragg/iStock; p. 4 StphaneLemire/iStock; p. 10 Mark Miller/Science Source; p. 13 Fox Searchlight/Everett Collection, Inc./Alamy Stock Photo; p. 14 and throughout Mika Besfamilnaya/Shutterstock; p. 15 SPUTNIK/Alamy Stock Photo; p. 19 Graylock/ABACAUSA.COM/Newscom; p. 20 Darren McCollester/Getty Images; p. 24 Paul Velgos/Shutterstock; p. 28 Nestor Rizhniak/Shutterstock; p. 30 Delphi234/Wikimedia Commons/File:US teen birth rate by state.svg/ CC PD; p. 34 Nina Robinson/The Verbatim Agency/The Packard Foundation/Getty Images; p. 36 Heather Stone/ KRT/Newscom; p. 38 Tyler Olson/Shutterstock; p. 40 gpointstudio/iStock; p. 43 Chaninny/Shutterstock; p. 48 Thomas Barwick/DigitalVision/Getty Images; p. 51 Imagesbybarbara/iStock/Getty Images; p. 54 Tina Stallard/ Getty Images; p. 58 Raquel Lonas/Moment/Getty Images; p. 59 Ksenia Sandulyak/Shutterstock; p. 63 Lee Roth/ Star Max via AP Images; p. 65 Courtney Hale/iStock; p. 70 Evso/Shutterstock.com; p. 72 ideabug/iStock/Getty Images; p. 75 Steve Russell/Toronto Star/Getty Images; p. 79 wavebreakmedia/Shutterstock; p. 83 Keith A Frith/ Shutterstock; p. 84 Michael Loccisano/RFK Human Rights/Getty Images; p. 89 digitalskillet/iStock/Getty Images; p. 92 DreamPictures/DigitalVision/Getty Images.

Printed in the United States of America

# CONTENTS

# Chapter 1

# Understanding Teen Pregnancy

Teen pregnancy is at an all-time low in the United States, down from the record high of almost 62 pregnancies for every 1,000 female teens in 1991 to just over 20 out of every 1,000 in 2016. This rate is dropping, even for those teens at the highest risk of unplanned pregnancy. Still, that number remains higher than those of many other developed countries, including Canada.

The high teen birth rate in the United States is not because American adolescents are having more

*Opposite*: Teens who experience pregnancy face a time of physical, emotional, and financial changes.

sex than teens elsewhere in the world. In fact, the majority of American high schoolers are not having sex. Instead, experts agree that there are complex reasons why the United States has such a high teen pregnancy rate.

Teen pregnancy rates are connected to access to health care, contraception, and sex education. Increasing access has lowered the rate. However, barriers remain. There is still a stigma and a lack of knowledge about sex, safe-sex practices, and options.

Teen pregnancy rates are also connected to life situations. Young people in struggling communities get pregnant at higher rates than do teens who believe they have options in life. Poverty, unstable home lives, and racism can make teens feel like they have only one path in life, or no path. They may not choose young parenthood, but they may not make choices (or be able to make choices) that prevent pregnancy.

Most teen pregnancies—some say 82 percent— are unplanned and unwanted. If pregnancy does happen, however, teen parents have options. The answers each parent chooses are personal ones that are right for that person. Babies of teen parents are not inferior to other children, and just because their parents did not expect them does not mean they are not loved. Teen parents are not less than their peers.

## PUBERTY AND FERTILITY

Teenagers have been having sex and getting pregnant since humanity began. Part of the reason for this is biological. Humans physically change from being children to being adults during puberty, and puberty starts for most people any time between age eight and age fourteen. During this stage in development, girls' and boys' bodies become physically able to reproduce. The hormones in both start to change. Hormones are chemicals that send messages to the body.

### Puberty in Females

Hormonal changes in girls lead to them to start their menstrual cycle. The menstrual cycle gets the body ready for pregnancy. During the menstrual cycle, a lot happens. The menstrual cycle usually includes menstruation, or getting a period. Each month, an egg develops in the ovaries. Once it is ready, it drops into one of the fallopian tubes and travels to the uterus, or womb. At the same time, the uterus's lining is building up. This lining, or wall, thickens so that if the egg is fertilized by a sperm during sex, it can attach to the wall and grow into a baby. If there is no fertilization, or pregnancy, the uterus's extra lining breaks down and leaves the girl's body in the form of blood. A period usually lasts two to seven days—this too varies from girl to girl and can vary from month to month for each girl. Then the cycle starts all over again. A person can become pregnant any time during her menstrual cycle. There is no "safe" time to have unprotected sex, not even during a period.

## Puberty in Males

The hormonal changes of puberty in boys lead to them to start producing sperm. The testicles nearly double in size during puberty and begin spermatogenesis, the production of sperm. About a year after the testicles enlarge, boys are able to procreate. Now, an erect penis can ejaculate, or expel, semen. This liquid contains sperm. When sperm combines with an egg, a human baby may grow. In every one teaspoonful of semen, there are two hundred million to five hundred million sperm. Just one of those hundreds of millions of sperm needs to connect with a female's egg for a pregnancy to happen.

## TEEN MINDS: NOT EMOTIONALLY READY TO REPRODUCE

While puberty readies people physically to reproduce, the changes during this stage of life make adolescents ill-prepared emotionally to have children. A teenager's brain is neither a child's brain nor an adult's brain. It is truly at an in-between stage, literally being renovated like a house under construction or a piece of software as it updates.

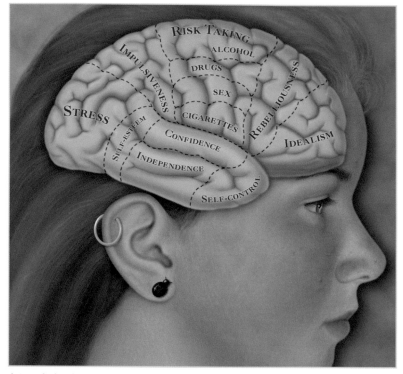

A teen's brain must manage a lot of new information and emotions.

The limbic system is the most active part of the changing adolescent brain. One of its major duties is to control emotions. Over the teen years, the prefrontal cortex slowly takes control of the limbic system. The ability to plan, control impulses, and think at a high level reins in emotions. Until that happens, teenagers feel a lot and feel strongly. Most humans naturally react to other people's expressions, but teenagers react the strongest of all ages. Brain scans prove this. All this emotional upheaval has an effect on the other brain changes that puberty brings.

Brain matter increases during adolescence, which helps teenagers start to figure things out and make decisions like adults do. These reasoning skills are new, though, and teens need more time than adults do to understand a situation. A decision made in the moment is likely to be more emotional than rational.

The new ability to think abstractly allows teens to study and to navigate social situations in new ways. Friends can start negotiating and compromising. Higher-level thinking also allows teens to consider themselves as others perceive them. That is why peer pressure is so powerful among adolescents. Teens become capable of thinking about what others think for the first time.

The adolescent brain feels rewarded when peers give their approval. It does not matter if that approval is for something positive or negative. Peer pressure can lead to teens doing positive things, like joining a school activity, or it can lead to taking dangerous risks. Risky behavior provides a rush of excitement in humans. To get the same level of excitement, teens need higher doses of risk than adults do.

Finally, hormone changes increase the number of receptors for oxytocin. In adults, this hormone is known as the bonding hormone. It helps adults want to interact with their romantic partners and their babies. In teenagers, oxytocin makes them feel self-conscious. Teens focus on how everyone connects with them, and this can lead to self-centered behaviors.

Making decisions based primarily on emotion, caring too much about the thoughts of peers (who are also in the midst of major physical and mental changes), feeling reward for taking risks, and focusing too much on the self are normal parts of being a teenager. They indicate that a person is transforming from a child into an adult. However, they also indicate that the person is not emotionally ready to care for a child.

# MEDIA PORTRAYALS OF TEEN PREGNANCY

Movies and television have a diverse and sometimes complicated track record of showing teen pregnancy. Researchers say these forms of entertainment play a role in the reality of teen pregnancy and birth rates.

## Movies

In the movies, perhaps no two films do a better job of showing Hollywood's contrasting ideas about

The movie *Juno* uses humor to talk about teen pregnancy.

teen pregnancy than *Juno* (2007) and *Precious* (2009). *Juno* approaches teen pregnancy with humor. Juno, the title character, becomes pregnant after having sex with her best friend. The quirky white high schooler weighs her options and decides to

# The Legacy of Maternity Homes

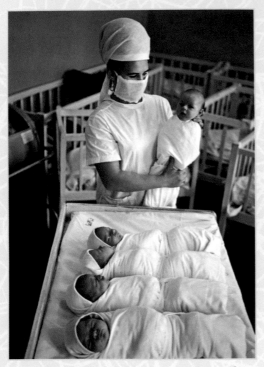

A midwife cares for the newborns of teen mothers living in a maternity home in the mid-1900s.

Becoming a teen parent is not the best idea for most people. It is not, however, a cause for stigma. Teen parents are humans who deserve respect, support, and rights. Tragically, society has not always treated young parents well.

From the mid-1940s to the early 1970s, more than a million and a half unmarried pregnant women in America were sent to so-called maternity homes and were forced to surrender their newborns to adoption.

Most of them were teenagers who had not had access to sex education or contraception. Pregnancy before marriage was considered something that did not happen to "good" families. Communities were told that the girls were sick and had to seek treatment out of town or that they were living with family members elsewhere. Really, the girls were in homes for unwed mothers. They could become visibly pregnant in private, and then they were pressured to choose adoption, so they could return home as though nothing in their lives had changed. In reality, everything had changed.

carry the baby to term. She pursues an open adoption with a loving, wealthy couple that desperately wants a baby. *Precious* was built around the distressing grit of being a teen mom. Precious, the title character, is a pregnant sixteen-year-old African American girl with one baby already. Her parents are abusive, her first baby has disabilities, and Precious is illiterate.

Surprisingly, *Juno* had a similar effect on teen viewers as *Precious* did. After *Juno* was nominated for four Oscars (it won Best Original Screenplay), the *Guardian* interviewed teenagers for their reactions. None of them, girls and boys ages fifteen and sixteen, viewed the characters' responses as realistic. Even though *Juno* made teen pregnancy look like a comedy, the teens weren't laughing at the truth behind the punchlines. "It made me much more scared about getting pregnant," one fifteen-year-old girl said.

## Television

Television shows are usually not built wholly around teen pregnancies, but many include pregnancy story lines. They handle these stories in different ways. *Glee*, about kids involved in high school musical theater, showed adoption via song-and-dance numbers, while *Parenthood*, a drama about a multigenerational family, offered an abortion storyline. *The Secret Life of the American Teenager* discussed one set of parents getting married and keeping their baby, a stillbirth for another, and all the other options and possibilities surrounding teen pregnancy.

One of the first television shows for teens that covered teen pregnancy was *Beverly Hills, 90210*. Gabrielle Carteris, who played high schooler Andrea Zuckerman, was twenty-nine and married when she became pregnant. The writers wrote her pregnancy into the show and then wrote her character out. While many people applauded the actor Carteris for her decision to both work and have a child, they also expressed frustration at the life the character Zuckerman was left to lead. She was passive about birth control and became pregnant after having sex with someone once. She considered abortion but chose to stay pregnant, marry the father, and start college, keeping her career goal of becoming a doctor. Many felt that the show was telling its young audience that teen pregnancy was easy to incorporate into life. There might be minor challenges, but on the whole, life can continue on schedule. In reality, bringing a child into the world massively changes life, even under the best of circumstances. Babies require great amounts of time, energy, and money that few teen parents have.

## Does Television Negatively or Positively Affect Teen Pregnancy Rates?

The media play a complicated role in teen pregnancy and birth rates. The first study to establish a link between teenagers watching sexual content on television and becoming young parents was published in 2008. The RAND Corporation published their findings in the journal *Pediatrics*. In 2001, the researchers asked two thousand adolescents about their television viewing and their sexual behavior.

They revisited those same people in 2002 and then in 2004. In a fourth survey, they talked with the seven hundred participants who had engaged in sexual intercourse by then. They found that when most of the television watched included a lot of sex scenes, the risk for teen pregnancy doubled compared to teens who did not watch mostly sex-focused television shows.

There is also evidence that television shows that speak openly about teen pregnancy can help lower teen birth rates. Researchers studied the effects of

*Teen Mom* stars Bristol Palin, Maci Bookout, and Farrah Abraham support the National Day to Prevent Teen Pregnancy.

# The Curious Case of the "Pregnancy Pact"

In 2008, a record number of students at Gloucester High School in Massachusetts experienced pregnancy.

In 2008, something strange happened in a tiny Massachusetts town: eighteen teens at Gloucester High School became pregnant. This figure was more than four times the number of pregnancies at the school in 2007.

The details behind these pregnancies were just as strange. Between October 2007 and May 2008, the school's nurse practitioner gave 150 pregnancy tests. Some of the students who received negative test results were disappointed they were not pregnant, and some of those who learned they were pregnant celebrated, gave each other high-fives, and started talking about planning baby showers.

According to the school's principal, half of the pregnant teens had made a so-called pregnancy pact to have and raise babies together. Experts in teen sex and reproduction said they had never before heard of teenagers making such a pact.

Not even two years later, the idea of a pact was considered untrue. Some of the girls said they were excited to get pregnant but not because they had made a promise to their friends. The reasons they, as well as the others, had unprotected sex were much more complicated. Many had unstable home lives, didn't think they were successful at anything, and were careless. The truth about what happened at Gloucester High wasn't a headline-grabbing story that could be easily explained. Instead, it showed the complicated and life-changing issues that teens and their families everywhere contend with.

the MTV network's reality show *16 and Pregnant*. Each episode, the cameras follow a different teen during and after pregnancy. Critics have said the show glamorizes caring for a newborn. A study released by the National Bureau of Economic Research in 2014 said that, in fact, the show led to a reduction in teen births by almost 6 percent. The researchers studied data from the eighteen months following the show's premiere. They noted a connection between locations with higher online searches and discussion about *16 and Pregnant* and higher searches and discussion about birth control and abortion. They also observed a connection between locations where a lot of people viewed *16 and Pregnant* and where there were big drops in teen births.

The results from both studies are not straightforward. The RAND study found several factors influenced teens becoming parents. Home life, race, and engagement in school were important, as was television watching. The researchers also recognized that television is one small part of a teen's media consumption. They called for further study of the connection between reproductive health and social media, music, and magazines. No one thinks *16 and Pregnant* (or its *Teen Mom* spin-offs) are wholly responsible for the decrease in teen births, but even the National Campaign to Prevent Teen and Unplanned Pregnancy (now Power to Decide) paid positive attention to the study's results.

## THE REALITIES OF TEEN PREGNANCY

Biology makes teen pregnancy possible, but it is rarely advisable. History has looked unfavorably on teen parents; modern society still does not always support teens in getting the reproductive health care and education they need. Media both mirrors the reality of teen pregnancy and twists it. For all these reasons and more, teen pregnancy is a thorny issue—and it is risky, for teens, babies, and society.

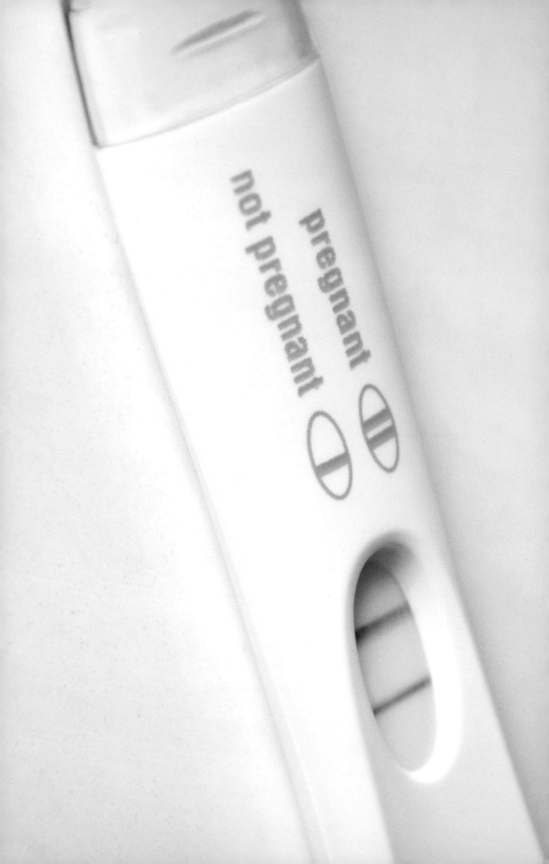

# Chapter 2

# The Risks of Teen Pregnancy

The answer to why teenagers find themselves facing a pregnancy is simple: they had unprotected sex, or their method of contraception failed. A sexually active adolescent who does not use contraception has a 90 percent chance of becoming pregnant or impregnating someone within a year. That is true whether the teen is black or white, rich or poor, living with both parents or not. Teen pregnancy is not limited to any particular group.

*Opposite*: Over-the-counter pregnancy tests from a pharmacy can be taken at home.

# DISPROPORTIONATE RISK

Though any teen can have their future altered by pregnancy, some teens are more likely to become young parents. Everyone who is sexually active and fertile can experience a pregnancy—and is taking a big risk that they will if they do not practice safe sex. However, the circumstances of some teenagers' lives mean they may be even more at risk. Teens living in poverty and who have a lack of options suffer the most, as do teens who do not have access to quality sex education. Those factors are often related to each other. Teens living in poor economic conditions often also have inadequate sex education programs.

## Health Care Disparity

Health care can be of lower quality in poor neighborhoods, towns, and regions. Teens in these places may struggle to access what medical care is available. They may not have insurance or money to pay for medical services. They may not have access to transportation to go to a doctor. They may not have time to go to a doctor because they are not only going to school but working at a job to help support their family.

## Economic Disparity

Teens living in areas with strong employment—where most adults have a job—are less likely to have a baby than are teens who grow up in poor economic conditions. Young people who cannot envision a positive future for themselves—one that includes college, a good job, or moving to an area with more choices—may see becoming parents as a path they must take. If young people, particularly young girls, do not expect to find employment that pays them enough to be financially independent, they may continue having children at a young age.

The economic cause of teen pregnancy means that certain regions of the country have higher youth pregnancy rates. Teens living in rural areas, where

# Pregnancy Prevention Is Not Always STI Prevention

Teen sexual health is about more than preventing pregnancy. A healthy teen makes smart choices that lead to strong relationships and do not lead to unplanned pregnancies and dangerous sexually transmitted infections (STIs). Just because a teen makes smart decisions about pregnancy prevention does not mean they are protected from STIs. Likewise, teens who make good decisions

Honest, open communication between partners is key to maintaining sexual health.

about preventing STIs may not be protecting themselves from unplanned pregnancy.

Abstaining from vaginal intercourse to prevent pregnancy or using birth control to prevent pregnancy do not always lower the risk of contracting an STI. Condoms are used as both birth control and STI prevention. However, all other forms of birth control, such as the pill and IUDs, prevent pregnancy only. They do nothing regarding STIs.

Many different types of sexual acts can transmit sexual diseases. Teens can prevent pregnancy and the spread of STIs by abstaining from all types of sex. If they are sexually active, they can lower their risk of both by using a safer-sex barrier made specifically for the type of sex they are engaging in. (It's a good idea for teens to make an appointment with a doctor to figure out what works best for their unique needs.) They can also get tested for STIs regularly and communicate honestly about pregnancy and illnesses with their parents, doctors, and sexual partners.

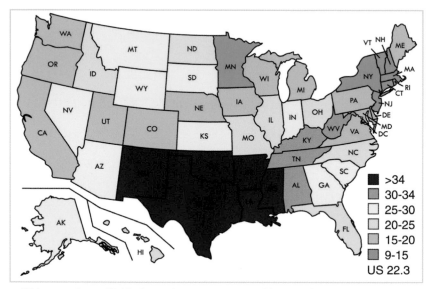

This map from 2015 shows how many teen girls out of every one thousand gave birth in each state.

there is less economic opportunity, are affected by pregnancies at a higher rate than are teens living in urban and suburban areas.

The link between finances and teen pregnancy also means that teens of color are disproportionately affected. Centuries of systemic racism in the United States have forced people of color into working for lower incomes and kept them there. More teen parents are Latinx or African American than white: 17 percent of Latinas, and 16 percent of African

American young women will give birth by the time they are twenty years old, while only 8 percent of white teens will.

## Education Disparity

Teens across the United States also receive unequal treatment when it comes to sex education programs. There is no standard for sex education across the United States. Abstinence always prevents pregnancy, but that does not mean that sex education is unnecessary. Teens with no sex education programs in school or abstinence-only sex education programs are at extra risk of being affected by pregnancy. They may know less about how sex leads to pregnancy and why it is wise to delay having sex. When they do have sex, they may not know why it is important to have fewer partners and how to correctly use protection.

Most of the country does not require that comprehensive sex education be taught. Twenty-seven states require programs to focus on abstinence, and eighteen states require schools teaching sex education to tell students that it is important to have sex only when married. Most states do not require students to take sex education classes at all. The number of students without access to sexual health education jumps when accounting for the many states that allow parents to remove their children from sex education classes.

Parental involvement is a good thing. Parents should have important discussions about sexual health at home. After all, researchers and teens alike consider parents the most important teachers of sexual health. Numerous studies show that teens whose parents talk with them about sex are more likely to choose to wait to have sex and use protection when they do have sex. Teens agree. In national surveys, most teens say they share their parents' values about sex and that their parents influence them above everything else. Parents talking honestly and regularly with them help them make healthy decisions. The Centers for Disease Control and Prevention (CDC) offers a resource for parents:

"Talking with Your Teens about Sex: Going Beyond 'the Talk.'"

Still, comprehensive sex education complements the education families give young people. Scientific evidence has overwhelmingly proved that the most effective school sex education programs teach students to delay having sex. These effective programs also teach students that when they do engage in sex, they should limit the number of partners they have, and they should always use protection correctly. Students of comprehensive sex education programs wait to have sex for the first time, have less sex with fewer people, and use birth control more than students who do not take these classes.

Teens across the country also receive varying information on topics related to sexual health.

Twenty-five states and the District of Columbia require school districts with sex education teach skills around expressing and receiving consent. Eleven states require guidance on how to talk to trusted adults, especially parents, about sex.

Teenagers in Mississippi learn about reproductive health.

Discussion of sexual orientation is an important part of sex education because teens of all identities benefit from sexual health. Most teen bodies go through standard biological development, so they have the capability of being involved in a pregnancy. If a sex education curriculum uses language that acknowledges only heterosexuality and cisgender identities (the sex assigned to a person at birth), students in other groups are more likely to tune out, assuming the information is not for them.

# SEXUAL HEALTH: OUTSIDE THE CLASSROOM

Even teens who receive high-quality sex education and have open and honest conversations with their parents might find themselves facing an unplanned pregnancy. If you've had unprotected sex or your contraception method fails, it's important to learn about what happens next.

## Determining if There Is a Pregnancy

Wondering if you are pregnant or if your partner is can be anxiety producing. This is a good time to start talking with trusted adults—especially if you are not already communicating about your sex life. It is not time to start panicking. Not every sexual encounter leads to a pregnancy. A missed period is an indication of pregnancy, but it is not a definitive one. Periods can be irregular, especially during the teen years, when the body is settling in to its new development stage. There may not be a pregnancy.

# Teens Advocating for Themselves

The metropolitan area of San Antonio, Texas, has one of the highest teen pregnancy rates in the United States. It is between 40 and 50 percent higher than the national rate for people ages fifteen to nineteen years old. Teens are working to change this.

A Texas teen holds her daughter.

Healthy Future Texas (HFTX) is a nonprofit organization based in San Antonio that uses education to try to prevent teen pregnancy. HFTX's Youth Advocacy Council (YAC) puts some of the power to keep teens healthy in the hands of teens themselves.

YAC members are in grades nine through twelve. They participate in outreach, education, and advocacy, sharing evidence-based sexual health education with both their peers and their state's lawmakers. They work on three major campaigns a year: Let's Talk Month in October, Teen Dating Violence Awareness in February, and National Month to Prevent Teen Pregnancy in May. They also participate in Advocacy Day, traveling to their state capital to talk with legislators about the importance of public policy regarding teen sexual health.

Taking a pregnancy test is a necessary step. The kind you buy at the store or get for free at a local clinic tests the urine for evidence of the hormone human chorionic gonadotropin (hCG) in the body. That hormone increases during the first few days of pregnancy. These tests are 97 percent effective—if used correctly.

If there is a negative result, but a woman's period still does not come, her breasts are tender, and she is especially tired, she should take a test again. She may also want to visit the doctor for a blood test, which also measures the presence of hCG.

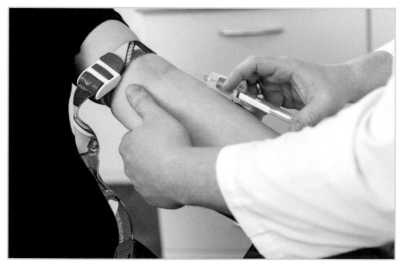

Doctors determine if patients are pregnant using a blood test.

Even if the pregnancy test is positive, the pregnancy may not be viable. An ultrasound—a full one with your doctor or a limited but free one at a clinic—can tell a lot. Some pregnancies are over almost as soon as they begin. A medical professional may determine there is a pregnancy, but it will end naturally and quickly without a baby starting to develop. If, however, there is a viable pregnancy, it is time to make choices and move forward.

## Risks of Pregnancy, Birth, and After the Delivery

Pregnancy is a natural part of life. However, that does not mean it is always safe and easy. Teen mothers are a group at high risk for a difficult pregnancy and birth. Just because a body is developed enough to become pregnant does not mean it can safely carry and birth a baby.

Even teen girls who have access to medical care often do not get adequate prenatal health care. Most pregnant teens were not planning to get pregnant, so they were not eating well and taking vitamins with pregnancy in mind. Certain nutrients can help prevent birth defects. Teens may not realize right away that they are pregnant, or they may be anxious about talking to doctors, so they may not make the medical appointments they should. Seeing a doctor early and getting regular screens for medical problems in the mother and baby will help address any new complications quickly.

Teens who get pregnant might also be facing other health conditions. Since they have not been practicing safe sex, they are more likely to engage in

Vitamins can help keep mothers and their unborn babies healthy.

a variety of risks. There is a higher rate of sexually transmitted infections (STIs) among teen parents. These can be transferred to the unborn child or cause other health issues in the fetus.

Additionally, pregnant teens are more likely to have high blood pressure than older moms are. This can combine with other biological issues to create preeclampsia, a dangerous condition that can cause everything from swelling to organ damage in the mom and disrupted growth and premature birth for the baby. The earlier a baby is born, the more the baby is at risk for troubles with breathing, digesting, seeing, and thinking.

Teens may be more at risk of experiencing obstructed labor, when the baby simply does not fit through the birth canal. This happens in teens because their bodies are not fully developed. For example, their hips may not be wide enough to accommodate a baby moving through.

All of these circumstances can lead to a dangerous situation for the baby, even after birth. Babies born to women of all ages in the United States are less likely to survive to their first birthday than babies in other wealthy countries. The number of babies who do not survive to their first birthday out of every one thousand babies born in a given year is called the infant mortality rate. Infant mortality is highest among teen moms. Experts believe this is due to a relatively high poverty rate in the United States as well as a weak social safety net (a collection of services provided by the government), and these are two issues that strongly affect teen moms.

Pregnant teens face emotional health risks too. They may be at higher risk for postpartum depression. Most new moms feel the "baby blues." It is normal to feel strange after giving birth. In addition to experiencing hormone shifts, new moms are not sleeping a lot and are dealing with an entirely different life than they had mere days before. If mood swings, sadness, or anxiety last more than a couple of weeks, the problem may be more serious. Depression can cause major problems for both the new mom and her baby.

There is no shame in postpartum depression. It affects many women. Anyone facing postpartum depression should reach out for help immediately. Depression is treatable, and there's no need to suffer in silence.

Pregnancy and birth are intense stages of life for everyone—full of physical and mental changes, new short-term and long-term plans, and uncertainties. This is especially the case for pregnant teens.

Talking with a mental health professional is helpful during pregnancy and after the birth.

However, once a person has become pregnant and has chosen to carry the baby to term, panicking and worrying are the least helpful actions to take. The best thing to do is take good care of your mind and body—and your baby's. Remember that the responsibility to protect yourself is always in your hands, and you can do this.

## ABORTION RISKS

Modern medicine has helped make pregnancy safer for the mother and the baby. Similarly, in modern America, abortions have been legalized and made relatively medically safe. When they are performed under the supervision of a licensed doctor, the physical side effects are few and rare. However, that does not make an abortion an easy response to pregnancy, especially for teens.

There are two types of abortions, medication and in-clinic. A pregnant person can choose to take pills early in the pregnancy to abort the fetus. Within the first ten weeks of pregnancy, this method is successful 93 to 98 percent of the time, depending on how early in the pregnancy it is used. The first pill is taken at the doctor's office, and the second pills are taken a day or two later. Usually about a day after that, the uterus releases the fetus, and the body pushes it out. This can all happen at home. What happens may not feel emotionally like a period, but it usually physically looks and feels similar to one. A person may continue to bleed a little and experience some cramping for a short time afterward.

Alternatively, a pregnant person can choose to undergo a surgical procedure in a medical office. This is 99 percent effective. It takes about ten minutes for a health-care professional, using gentle suction and a curet (a sharp, spoon-shaped tool), to remove the fetus. There is always physical risk involved with any surgery. In this case, it is possible for there to be slight damage to the wall of the uterus. This could make it difficult to get pregnant in the future. Undergoing multiple abortions can also damage the body for future pregnancies.

Both kinds of abortions require a lot of time, talking, and paperwork. A pregnant person must discuss abortion and options with health-care providers before she is allowed to make an appointment for one. Sometimes, these must be done on different dates. There's a physical exam and lab tests before and recovery time and follow-up doctor visits after. For teens, there is even more restriction. Thirty-seven states require adult parents to be involved in a teen's decision to have an abortion. In twenty-one states, this requires the adult parent to agree to their teen having an abortion. In some states, it is possible to use a judge's permission instead of a parent's, but appearing before the court and getting this judicial bypass takes time. The physical risks possible from an abortion increase the longer a person is pregnant.

Still, the choice is up to the mother, not to her parents, friends, or even the other person involved in the pregnancy. It is a good, if difficult, idea if a pregnant teen asks herself some questions:

- How would having a baby change my life or my future in ways I do and do not want?

- How would having an abortion change my life or my future in ways I do or do not want?

- Would I consider adoption?

- Would it "feel right" to me to choose abortion?

- Is anyone pressuring me to have or not have an abortion?

- What kind of support would I need and what kind would I get if I decided to have a baby? What if I chose an abortion instead?

About 18 percent of all abortions in the United States end a teen pregnancy. Still, the rate of abortions among adolescents is the lowest since abortion became legal. It is 76 percent lower now than in 1988, when the rate of teen abortions was at a historic high. Many teens are making other choices about pregnancy.

# Chapter 3

# Experiencing Teen Pregnancy

The majority of teens who become parents are eighteen or nineteen years old. However, the younger a person becomes sexually active, the more likely they will face a pregnancy. Experts say that 22 percent of boys who have had sex before age fifteen have also been involved in a pregnancy. That number jumps to 46 percent for young girls with the same sexual experience.

When Daizchane Baker was fourteen years old, she was enjoying getting started in her high school

*Opposite*: It's important to schedule regular appointments with your doctor during pregnancy.

life. Then she learned from her doctor that she was four months pregnant. She wrote in an article for *Teen Vogue*:

> **The thought of being responsible for another person when I could barely take care of myself really scared me. I was disappointed because I knew the plans I had for my future would be hindered by a child. My mom and dad were disappointed too, since they had been teen parents themselves. They didn't want me to experience what they had to go through.**

Baker feared she was about to become a statistic. The research shows that Baker's fears were not unreasonable. Education and career goals change once teens become parents, and it is not unusual for the children of people who were teen parents to also become pregnant teens. Like all teens involved in a pregnancy, Baker was about to face serious consequences.

# EDUCATION CONSEQUENCES

Getting pregnant is the leading cause of girls dropping out of high school. More than 50 percent of teen mothers never graduate. Even those who earn their degree do not progress much further. Regardless of whether they graduate high school, less than 2 percent of girls who became parents in high school earn a college degree by the time they turn thirty.

Being pregnant or being the father of a baby will affect your schooling. You may have to miss school occasionally to see the doctor, and if the due date is during the school year, you likely will miss school for that. If you are the girl,

Pregnant teens must work hard to prioritize their education.

you may experience physical symptoms that interfere without warning, like morning sickness that sends you running from class to the bathroom. You may have to quit sports you are in or cut the season short.

The key to navigating this is communication. Ask your school counselor, principal, and teachers if the school has a plan for working with pregnant teens. Tell them what your needs and concerns are. If there are major obstacles that cannot be addressed to everyone's satisfaction, teen moms may have to consider transferring to a school specially designed for pregnant teens, taking classes online, or working toward a GED at their own speed at home.

## SOCIAL CONSEQUENCES

Taking online classes is one schooling option that pregnant teens can consider if they find it hard to attend in-person classes. This may help pregnant teens stay more consistent with their learning, but it may negatively affect their social life. Teen parents studying online will not see their friends every day. The difficulty in making and keeping friends often continues after childbirth. A teen's focus must move to the newborn child, leaving little time, or resources, for spending with friends.

That does not mean that life is over. Many teens work hard to graduate high school—finishing their classes online or putting their babies in day care so that they can return to classes. If they go on to college, their experiences will be different in many ways from the average college student's. For one thing, they will not be able to live in the dorms. However, they can be "normal" college kids in other ways. Many teen parents participate in honors programs and  extracurricular activities.

## THE FATHER'S INVOLVEMENT

Pregnancy, especially an unplanned one, can put a lot of stress on even the strongest of relationships. Teen mothers and fathers often break up, either during

A nineteen-year-old dad cares for his newborn child.

the pregnancy or soon after the birth. Eight out of ten teen couples who have a baby together do not stay together romantically.

Teen fathers may not even stay in the picture at all or may participate in just some aspects of their baby's lives. Like teen moms, teen dads are less likely to finish high school than their classmates who are not parents. They also are more likely to be economically disadvantaged and to struggle with finding good work. These challenges are likely to negatively affect their child's life. Unlike teen moms, teen dads have an easier time ignoring their responsibilities and often do. The law supports this in that an unmarried father needs to take legal action to obtain parental rights and responsibilities. However, there is growing evidence that teen dads want to be involved in their children's lives.

David was eighteen years old when he learned his seventeen-year-old girlfriend was pregnant. He came from a family in which the kids were expected to go to college before they started families of their own. Instead of ignoring his new role as teen father, he embraced it. He told WashingTeenHelp, which helps pregnant and parenting teens in Washington State with information and resources, "I couldn't let [my girlfriend] go with the pregnancy alone, I had to go through everything with her."

*MEL* magazine interviewed teen dads from different generations about their experiences. They all experienced serious challenges. Craig was a happy senior in high school, and he had a baseball scholarship to college. Then his girlfriend of eight months became pregnant. They decided to get married and raise the child. Craig quit school and was working fifty hours a week. He was an adult when other people his age were still kids. By the time he was only twenty-three, he had two kids, a career, a house, and was divorced.

Zachary was seventeen years old when the girl he had known for a week got pregnant. All he could think about was his own father. For the first year and a half of Zachary's life, his dad rejected his new role. His dad eventually accepted his responsibility, and when Zachary put himself in a similar situation, his dad advised him to step up as well.

## FAMILIES OF TEEN PARENTS

Teen pregnancies can "run in the family." Children of teen parents are more likely than their peers to become teen parents themselves. Daughters of teen mothers are 66 percent more likely to get pregnant when they are teenagers.

That happened to Jessica Chester. Her mother and her grandmother had been teen moms too. At seventeen, Chester did not seem likely to get pregnant—she had a 4.5 GPA and a full-tuition scholarship to college. She and her boyfriend were not, however, using birth control regularly. She became pregnant in her senior year of high school. She finished her studies and kept her scholarship, all while being pregnant and giving birth. Then her life again matched the statistics, and she got pregnant again.

## REPEAT PREGNANCIES

About 25 percent of teen moms get pregnant again within two years of having their first baby. Three months after Jessica Chester's first baby was born, Chester was still a star student, this time a full-time college student with a double major—and she was carrying her second child.

Some teen parents have more than one child.

She and her boyfriend had not realized she could get pregnant so soon after giving birth. Her high school had offered abstinence-only sex education. Furthermore, Chester's mother had not been comfortable discussing sex, even though since she had been a teen mom herself, she had a lot of useful information to share.

Some states' policies make it difficult to prevent second pregnancies. In Texas, teenagers usually need a parent's permission to get birth control—even if they are already parents themselves.

# FINANCIAL CONSEQUENCES

It is not impossible for teen parents to complete their schooling, but it does require having a new perspective on money. Most teen parents, even those who have help from their families, must work or take out loans to pay for day care. Unlike many of their peers, whose main job is doing well in school, teen parents have two jobs: doing well in school and

Preparing for a baby involves buying clothes, diapers, bottles, and much more.

raising a child. Being a teen parent usually means adding a third, paid job to this already full schedule.

In 2017, experts estimated that raising a child from birth through age seventeen costs lower-income households $175,000. The first big expense is the delivery. Insurance or Medicaid, which is a government-funded health services program for people with limited incomes, can help pay for the cost of childbirth. If you are uninsured or do not have Medicaid, a delivery without complications can cost $7,600 to $13,500, depending on where you live. Private insurance cuts those prices by about $4,000.

Many baby supplies, like a stroller, crib, and changing table, can be bought used or borrowed. That helps to lower costs a little. Some things need to be new. Car seats have expiration dates and should not be trusted as 100 percent safe unless they are brand new. Those cost $80 to $500. Clothes and diapers are estimated to cost about $750 a year for the baby's first two years. Food is another $1,500 each year. "Inexpensive" childcare can cost nearly $3,000 per year. Housing costs also go up with a child. A single adult can live in one small room, but it is more difficult, and often impossible, to do that with a baby. As the child grows, some costs will be lost—for example, the stroller will not be needed forever. Other costs will grow or be added. Food costs will increase the older a child becomes, and this estimated total does not include any help with college costs.

Eighteen-year-old Shantay Newman, mother to a nineteen-month-old baby, told the Pennsylvania news source *Penn Live*, "I still wake up in the middle of the night crying and thinking, 'This is crazy.' You get up early, you feed the baby, you go to school, you pick the baby up, you feed the baby, you clean up after the baby, you wash clothes, you worry if you have enough money for diapers."

Babies cost society a lot too. Each year, teen pregnancies in Texas, a state with one of the highest youth pregnancy rates, cost the state over $1 billion. Some of that is spent on social services that teen

# Solange's Story

Solange Knowles was first known as the younger sister of Beyoncé, but she has become a powerful recording artist in her own right. She was also a teen mom.

For the May 2017 *Teen Vogue* cover story about her, Solange wrote a letter to her younger self. In it, she opened up about her pregnancy. She wrote (lowercase letters intentional):

seventeen will be the hardest year of your life. it will grow you up almost immediately.

you will be terrified ... some people will count you out because of the decision you've made to bring another life into the world so young, but you made the decision out of love and will live with the decision in love.

When Solange welcomed her son with her then-husband, her singing career was also just beginning. She told *Us Weekly* that it was "one of the most bittersweet moments" of her life. She felt such love for her son and wanted to be with him constantly, but it was difficult to care for a newborn and a new career. "It was isolating

Solange Knowles became a mother in 2004.

and lonely," she said. She had a husband, a supportive family, and fame and money, and it was still, she said, "hard to imagine being able to progress in my career in any way."

parents use, and some of that number includes the state's loss in revenue because teen parents do not usually work the higher paying jobs they would have gotten had they stayed in school.

# THE EXPERIENCE OF CHILDBIRTH

Teen parents face steep consequences, but successful outcomes are possible. Knowing what to expect from childbirth and early childcare can set you up for success.

## Contractions

Labor contractions signal that a pregnant person will soon give birth. This movement in the womb helps to push the baby out. Every pregnancy is unique. One mother in her twenties told *Cosmopolitan*: "All the things you think birth will feel like will be wrong. I read all the books and thought I was so prepared, but it was way different than what I expected. It was much easier than I expected in some ways, but

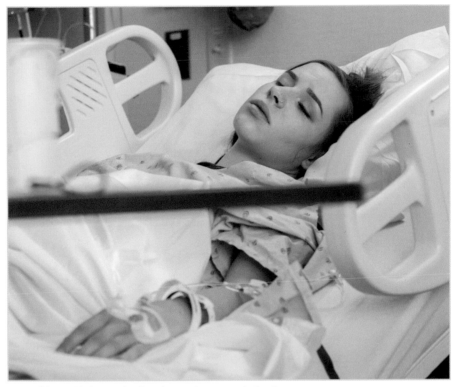

Giving birth can be hard on a teenager's body.

also a lot harder in other ways." Some people move through it relatively easily. All experience some level of discomfort, and many find it a painful experience.

Media website *The Cut* asked people to describe what having contractions felt like to them. Some of their answers were vivid: having a contraction was like "throwing up in reverse"; "like food poisoning x 1,000";

# It's Important to Understand Every Body

Teen pregnancy affects everyone— teens who identify as cisgender (their gender identity matches their sex assigned at birth); transmasculine (assigned at birth as female and identifying as male); transfeminine (assigned at birth as male and identifying as female); and nonbinary (not identifying throughout life as either female or male). What is different among these groups is that until recently, researchers have focused their efforts on understanding pregnancy rates in cisgender teens only.

It is becoming increasingly common for teens to identify as a gender different from the sex listed on their birth certificate. Researchers estimate that one in 137 teens age thirteen to seventeen years old in the United States identifies as transgender.

In 2014, researchers from the University of British Columbia and other Canadian institutions conducted the Canadian Trans Youth Health Survey. They talked with one thousand people ages fourteen to twenty-five who identify as transgender.

They found that transgender and cisgender youth have the same needs for education about teen pregnancy. Transgender teens do have sex, and even those people taking hormones to transition their genders are not necessarily infertile, as had been believed.

People writing sex education curricula have not usually considered trans teens as part of the audience. Gendered language can make them feel left out and like the information is not relevant to them. If they do not pay attention to information on sexual health, they may be more at risk for becoming pregnant.

and "like gnomes squeezing my abdomen with a hot vise." One mother said that experiencing hours of childbirth was actually easier for her, physically and mentally, than months of pregnancy.

## The First Days with Baby

Like any extreme physical experience does, giving birth also sends the body into an adrenaline high. This helps the new mom take care of her baby—biology says she needs to be awake and feeling well enough to feed her baby.

Eventually, this feeling of wakefulness wears off. All those muscles that tensed up during labor start to ache, just like they do after a tough gym class or a grueling sports practice. If the labor did some damage to the mom's body, which is often the case, her healing wounds may start to make walking, sitting, or lying down uncomfortable. At the same time the mother is feeling drained, the new baby is feeling anything but tired. Newborns are as unique as pregnancies and labors are—each one is different—but many want to eat every two to three hours. Being a parent changes a teen's life immediately: there is no such thing as a weekend or a school break after childbirth.

## BREASTFEEDING AND PUMPING

A mom who cannot breastfeed or who chooses not to is not a bad mom. Feeding a baby formula may be the best idea for a particular baby and mom. Even moms who breastfeed sometimes supplement the milk their bodies produce with formula.

That said, choosing to breastfeed has a lot of benefits. Breast milk contains the right balance of nutrients for a baby and antibodies to help keep a baby healthy. It is the food that newborns can most easily digest. Breastfeeding might even help the mom lose some of the weight she put on during pregnancy. Finally, breast milk is affordable—a mom's body naturally produces it, no coupons required.

Breastfeeding is often portrayed as a soft, loving activity. It does help the mother and child bond,

Mothers decide between breastfeeding, pumping, giving their babies formula, or a combination of the three.

physically and emotionally, but it is anything but gentle. Even those women who say it feels good acknowledge that it is an intense experience. As breasts fill with milk, they become heavy and achy. All mothers, including those who are not breastfeeding, must empty their breasts—either by feeding her baby or by using a pump to extract the milk. *The Cut* interviewed several women about what breastfeeding feels like. Some had positive experiences, but many thought the activity was less than fun. One mother said, "At first, I had sharp pains as if someone was using a Shop-Vac on my [breast]." Another said simply, "Breastfeeding is boring." Another mom said, "The right latch is like a thousand tiny super-magnets. A bad latch, though, is body-curling pain, like sandpaper on bleeding wounds, and you have to keep doing it over and over because newborns nurse all the time."

Life changes with pregnancy, no matter what happens—there is no doubt about that. There are physical, emotional, social, and financial changes, some of which will never again return to what they were. The good news is there is always hope.

# Chapter 4

# Hope and the Future

Teens are rewriting their own stories when it comes to pregnancy. They are making choices that improve their lives, as well as their children's. For a teen parent, wishing you had not faced a pregnancy does not mean that your child is not lovable or worthy of life—just as loving your child does not mean you are glad you had a baby so young.

Vivian Rivera's mom was eighteen when she gave birth to Vivian. Thirteen years later, Vivian gave birth to her own daughter. In an interview with

*Opposite*: With support, teen parents and their babies can thrive.

her hometown newspaper in central Pennsylvania, Vivian turned to her daughter, who was by then seven years old, and said, "It stops here." The cycle of teen pregnancy in their family was going to stop. Vivian was going to do everything she could to prevent her daughter from also being a teen parent.

## ADULT SUPPORT

Breaking the cycle of teen pregnancy seems to be important to people across the country. Even though rates of young pregnancies in the United States are still too high, the number continues to decline. Beyond the work teens themselves are doing, adults from across the political and social spectrum also seem to want to support positive change.

Eighty-five percent of adults want the federal government to continue funding programs proven to help teens abstain from sex and also use contraception often and correctly. People from both main political parties agree. Research shows that 89 percent of

Young people protest in favor of sex education.

Democrats want this funding to continue, and 75 percent of Republicans do. The majority of adults—79 percent—believe teens should receive more information about both abstinence and birth control. Experts say 81 percent of Democrats and 73 percent of Republicans believe in this kind of comprehensive sex education.

# Emergency, Crisis, and Support Resources

If you or a person you are with are in immediate danger, call 911. If you need someone to talk to about pregnancy, adoption, or an emotional crisis, there are plenty of people ready to help.

## ADOPTION HOTLINE

Get information and support twenty-four hours a day, seven days a week, with no obligation to pursue adoption.

**800-ADOPTION**

## ALL-OPTIONS TALKLINE

Volunteer peer counselors take calls from people who are pregnant as well as their loved ones. They discuss all options and responses to pregnancy and supporting someone who is pregnant.

**888-493-0092**

Monday-Friday 10:00 a.m.–1:00 a.m. Eastern Time Zone

Saturday-Sunday 10:00 a.m.–6:00 p.m. Eastern Time Zone

## BABY SAFE HAVEN

This confidential, toll-free hotline is for people who are pregnant and do not feel they can care for their baby or people who already have a baby they feel they cannot care for.

**888-510-BABY (888-510-2229**)

## PLANNED PARENTHOOD

Call to get counseling and referrals.

**800-230-PLAN (800-230-7526)**

## TEEN LINE

Teen volunteers (with the supervision of adult mental health providers) offer support and information.

**310-855-HOPE (310-855-4673) or**

**800-TLC-TEEN (800-852-8336)**

6:00–10:00 p.m. Pacific Time Zone

Text TEEN to 839863

6:00–9:00 p.m. Pacific Time Zone

## School Support

Sexual education in school is important, but it is most effective if it works with students' families and communities. Some school districts are starting to respond to this nuance. Here are just a couple examples of effective and innovative sex education programs that are both scientifically and medically accurate as well as supportive of community needs.

*¡Cuidate!* is a sex education program tailored to Spanish-speaking students. In English, it is called Take Care of Yourself. Using mainstream Latino cultural beliefs and proven science as its framework, its goal is to increase students' ability to talk about abstinence and condom use with their girlfriends and boyfriends.

Big Decisions is a curriculum being used in more than twenty school districts in Texas. It is considered an abstinence-plus curriculum, meaning it encourages waiting to have sex but also provides information to prevent pregnancy and STIs in case a teen chooses to have sex.

## PEER SUPPORT

The open and honest support of trusted adults—parents and educators—helps teens make wise decisions and stay healthy. Friends help too, and sometimes they are the first people a teen turns to when they are scared or worried. Sometimes, if you notice your friend is in trouble, you may want to speak up first.

The advice of good friends can help prevent pregnancy, and friends can also offer support if pregnancy happens.

If you have a friend who is having unprotected sex, consider reaching out to them. Ask them to talk—in person—in a private, quiet place where you won't be interrupted. You are not there to lecture them; you are there because you care. You can also offer your friend more than just a listening ear. One of the most useful things you can talk about as a friend is birth-control options. Every method of birth control is safer than an unplanned teen pregnancy.

Sometimes teens who are interested in the birth-control pill will ask to borrow a friend's extra pills. This is not a safe thing to do. One, there is no such thing as "extra pills," if a person is using the birth control correctly. Pills must be taken daily. Two, pills are prescription medicine, and prescriptions should never be shared. Each body reacts differently with medicine. The pill is safe for most, but only a health-care professional can determine which brand of pill, if any, is the right one.

Condoms are effective and available over-the-counter—no doctor's appointment necessary. They are even available for free in some clinics and school nursing centers. If they are unopened, undamaged, and within their expiration date, they are even safe to share. You can ask for a friend's extra condom.

The American Academy of Pediatrics recommends intrauterine devices (IUDs) and long-acting reversible contraception (LARC) for teens. These two devices—both of which a doctor implants inside the body—are the most effective forms of birth control. They bring the likelihood of pregnancy down to almost zero, and they last for years. No remembering to take a daily pill or making sure you have a condom nearby.

This is a lot of information, much of which your friend needs to talk about with their parents and doctor. However, as a peer who understands what your friend is experiencing, you can make a difference by starting the conversation.

## ADOPTION

If a friend comes to you because they have learned they are pregnant, your support remains invaluable.

Part of the reason so many teen pregnancies are unplanned is because many teenagers do not view themselves as the type of kids who will get pregnant. That can make thinking about raising a child or having an abortion extra shocking. Life suddenly feels like it will change in a big way. With you by their side, they can start to think through all the options. One option worth considering is adoption. With adoptions, teens do not have to face the possible challenges of getting an abortion as a minor, and they also do not have to make a lifelong commitment to parenting another human when their own lives are just beginning.

Fifteen-year-old Haley was one such teen. She was an honors student in high school, where she also had a solid group of friends. She was on the school's dance team and active in her church. Her mom was a single mom with a full-time job. Because she was so busy and because her children had always made smart choices, she trusted them, and they trusted themselves. Haley had never planned on having sex before marriage, and then she did. She became pregnant, something else she of course had never anticipated happening before marriage. Her mom told her she would support whatever Haley wanted to do. Haley chose adoption.

## Adoption Basics

If you are considering adoption, it is a good idea to first seek out an adoption lawyer or an adoption agency to help you through this process. You can do this as soon as you decide adoption is the route

Adoption can be a good choice for some pregnant teens.

# Celebrities Who Made an Adoption Plan

When Kate Mulgrew got pregnant at the start of her acting career, she decided on adoption.

When celebrities adopt a child, they generate a buzz. Some celebrities chose adoption for children they give birth to. That is talked about less but is still newsworthy.

Kate Mulgrew, an actor on the television shows *Star Trek: Voyager* and *Orange Is the New Black*, was twenty-one years old when she chose adoption for her baby. It was 1977, and she was playing the lead role on a popular daytime soap opera. Mulgrew chose to continue with the pregnancy even though she had no support from her family or the baby's father, who wanted her to have an abortion, and even though being pregnant could have harmed her young career. Mulgrew made an adoption plan.

Jay Thomas was an Emmy Award–winning comedian who was also just beginning his career when his girlfriend became pregnant. They talked honestly with each other about what to do. They considered abortion. They also considered having the baby and getting married, but they did not see a long-term future together. They decided on adoption.

For about twenty years, Mulgrew and Thomas both built their careers. They also started their own families—once they were ready. They each had two more children, and they both ended up having positive reunions with the children they had placed for adoption.

for you and the baby. It is never too early in the pregnancy. These experts will help you move through the process correctly and will help you through any challenges that may happen. You will not pay for these services; the family who adopts your baby will.

Then you will develop an adoption plan. You will choose an adoptive family and how much contact you want to have with that family before and after the adoption. All adoptive parents have been screened by the state they live in, so you know they have met state standards of safety, but you may want to know more about their interests, lifestyles, and personalities. Your attorney or agency will help you get this information.

There are two types of adoptions, closed and open. Closed adoptions keep your information secret from the adoptive parents and the baby you will place with them. You and the parents talk only through lawyers. There is no contact after the adoption. The amount of information shared and contact had between the adoptive family and you during open adoptions varies.

You may provide just your name and your hometown, for example, or you and the parents may stay in contact and you may be a part of your child's life. It is important to be flexible about this. How much contact the adoptive parents want, you want, and the child wants may change over time.

If you choose adoption, your baby will not go into foster care. Foster care is for children of parents who want to be reunited with their children when their own life situation improves. If a parent is choosing to give up their parental rights and choosing adoption, that child will go to another family, usually of that parent's choice.

You can change your mind until you sign away your rights, which happens after the birth. It is understandable if you doubt your decision. It is a big choice to make. Also, the hormonal, emotional, and physical changes you are going through during pregnancy can make you feel one decision is correct in one moment, and in the next, you may think a different path is right for you and your baby. Working with a mental health counselor is a good idea, as is being open and honest with your adoption lawyer or agency.

## HOW TO COPE AND THRIVE

If you are facing a pregnancy, you are about to experience many changes and decisions, big and small. Here are just a few things you can do to make a lot of difference.

### Ask for Help

When you are a teenager trying to make decisions about a baby and maybe trying to raise one, you are going to need help with money, transportation, managing your time, and trying to meet your life goals. If you are the mother, having a trusted adult in your life can help you eat well, exercise safely, get plenty of rest, and go to the doctor—all things you need to do to stay healthy yourself and help your baby develop in a healthy way. If you are the father, it is important for you to help the baby's mother. You

Trusted adults can help teens stay healthy and make the choices that are right for them.

are not supporting a life growing inside you, but you are supporting the mother of your child.

Talking with your parents can be difficult under the best of circumstances. If you are a teen parent, you may have lost their trust. Do little things to earn it back over time. Keep track of the doctor's appointments and parenting classes. Help around the house. Continue telling them the truth. Some parents react in a strongly negative way to a teen pregnancy. If the situation is really bad with your parents, seek help from another trusted adult.

Also reach out to your friends. If you are pregnant, you are going to be more tired than usual, and you are going to have deeper mood swings than most teenagers. Your hormones are changing even more than other teens' hormones are. Do not let that keep you from your friends. Talk to them about what you are experiencing and work with them to plan short activities.

Whenever possible, keep an open line of honest communication with the other parent of your child. Unfortunately, unplanned teen pregnancies can too often come from negative relationships. If there is any abuse in your relationship, talk with an adult. If you feel safe with the other parent, stay connected to them. Even if you were in a committed relationship before the pregnancy, do not be surprised if things feel strained sometimes. A pregnancy changes even the most stable of relationships. Remember that not every question or idea has to be answered or discussed in one conversation. For example, you don't have to answer the question about marriage in the first conversation, and you may not know for a long time the answers to the questions "Will she be a good mom?" "Will he be a good dad?"

If you need to, call a confidential hotline. Speaking honestly can feel scary in the moment, but it will help in the long term. You do not need to go through this by yourself, and you are never alone. If you call a hotline, be prepared for them to ask you a few questions before you begin talking, like your name and age. The conversation is still confidential. They just need to know what to call you, and they need basic statistics for research and fundraising purposes.

## Get Early Prenatal Care

Call your doctor as soon as you think you might be pregnant. Talk to your doctor about taking folic acid. This form of B vitamin helps prevent some birth defects. Do not be afraid to ask your school nurse or counselor to help you if you do not have a doctor or are worried about cost. They can help you find low-cost resources.

Teens can meet their education goals even as they parent a child.

Do not drink alcohol, smoke tobacco, or take drugs. They are even more harmful to the fetus growing inside of you than they are to you. Talk to your doctor if you would have trouble quitting any of these substances.

## Make Education a Priority

Parenthood is the number-one reason why teen girls do not finish high school. Dropping out to care for a newborn does not have to be where their education story ends. DoSomething.org helps young people across the United States and around the world to volunteer, campaign, and start organizations that improve society. One of their programs is the Babysitters Club. Teens can sign up to provide free babysitting services to parents who are taking GED classes. The General Educational Development (GED) exam is a test people who do not finish high school the traditional way can take to earn a high school diploma. Before pregnancy is even an issue, be engaged with school and after-school activities.

Busy teens who are interested in and finding success in academics, the arts, and sports are less likely than other adolescents to face an unplanned pregnancy.

## THE POWER OF POSITIVE ACTION

Teen pregnancy rates are at their lowest in the history of the United States. Yet media shows teen sex more than ever. As a twentysomething, Alyssa Rosenberg wrote for online publication *IndieWire* that screenwriters "move television further away from real teens' experiences … They treat teenagers like they're more irresponsible than actual American teenagers prove to be." However, the teen pregnancy rate in the United States remains one of the highest among wealthy countries. The numbers are as complex as the issue itself: there is no one type of teen who becomes pregnant, no one response to teen pregnancy that is right for everyone, and no one experience that all teens involved in a pregnancy will have. This experience is incredibly personal.

There is, however, research collected over the decades that is helping guide adults and teens alike toward stronger, smarter choices, plans, and responses. We know who is most at risk of becoming involved in a teen pregnancy. We also know that access to comprehensive sex education at home and in school, birth control, school and career opportunities, and quality health-care options lower that risk. Each of us has a responsibility to continue to lower the teen pregnancy rate and better support teens whose lives are changed by pregnancy.

# Glossary

**abstinence** Refraining from engaging in sex.

**abstinence-only sex education** Programs that only teach students not to have sex and do not teach them about protection from pregnancy and sexually transmitted infections. Also called abstinence-only-until-marriage (AOUM) and, since 2018, sexual risk avoidance.

**birth control** Something that prevents or lessens the frequency of conception.

**birth defects** Problems that develop before a baby is born.

**closed adoption** An adoption in which the adoptive family does not know identifying information about the birth parents. In some cases, the birth parents do not know information about the adoptive family.

**contraception** Deliberate prevention of conception; also known as birth control.

**disparity** A big difference between people or things.

**disproportionate** Out of proportion; too large or too small compared with something else. If a group of people experience something more or less than other groups do, they experience it disproportionately.

**fertile** Able to reproduce.

**hormones** Messenger chemicals that tell the body's processes, including sexual function and reproduction, to turn on or off.

**judicial bypass** A legal process that allows a judge to make decisions on the behalf of teens, instead of their parents.

**limbic system** A complex system of nerves and networks in the brain that controls emotions and urges like wanting to eat, have sex, and take care of others.

**menstrual cycle** A monthly set of activities in the female body, including menstruation, or the period, that allows the person to reproduce.

**open adoption** Any relationship between an adoptive family and birth parents in which they share information about their identities and communicate directly with each other.

**postpartum depression** A diagnosable condition that involves severe and longer-lasting depression after childbirth than the "baby blues."

**prefrontal cortex** The part of the brain responsible for higher-level thinking like planning, judging, weighing options.

**prenatal care** Health care during a pregnancy.

**procreate** Reproduce; create a new human.

**protection** Device used during sex to prevent pregnancy or sexually transmitted infections.

**puberty** The stage of life when young people gain the ability to reproduce.

**safe sex** Having sex while taking precautions against health risks.

**sperm** A type of cell produced by male sex organs.

**spermatogenesis** The production of sperm.

**STI** Sexually transmitted infections; now used more commonly than the term "sexually transmitted diseases" (STDs).

**stigma** Unfair feelings of shame that are associated with sensitive topics.

**term** The medically standard length of a pregnancy. A baby is considered preterm if they are born before thirty-seven weeks.

**ultrasound** An imaging technique that doctors use to examine an unborn baby. Ultrasounds are not invasive and do not hurt.

**uterus** Another word for womb; the place where a baby is conceived and where it grows.

**viable pregnancy** A pregnancy that should end in childbirth, if the parents choose to maintain it.

# Further Information

## BOOKS

De Meza, Lesley, and Stephen De Silva. *A–Z of Growing Up, Puberty, and Sex*. New York: Franklin Watts, 2019.

Fonda, Jane. *Being a Teen: Everything Girls & Boys Should Know About Relationships, Sex, Love, Health, Identity & More*. New York: Random House, 2014.

Koya, Lena. *Teen Pregnancy and What Comes Next*. Women in the World. New York: Rosen Publishing, 2018.

## WEBSITES

**Squires**

https://www.squirespdx.org

Founded by a former teen dad, Squires offers education, mentorship, and other resources for dads ages fourteen to twenty-five.

**Stay Teen**

https://stayteen.org

A program of Power to Decide, a campaign to prevent unplanned pregnancy, Stay Teen offers science-based information to young people, so they can make their own informed decisions. They also seek contributions of articles, essays, videos, and more by thirteen-to-nineteen-year-olds.

## VIDEOS

### The Story of a Teen Father

https://www.youtube.com/watch?v=Pbcf_oXw59o
Edwin Olguin talks about when he and his girlfriend found out she was pregnant and what it has been like to be a teen father.

### Teen Mom Nation: A Cycle of Teen Pregnancy

https://www.youtube.com/watch?v=ys4FEFphRYE
Lisa Ling tells the story of a family who has experienced teen pregnancy across two generations and their day-to-day struggles.

# Bibliography

Abraham, Yvonne. "No Picnic for Teen Mothers." *Boston Globe*, February 28, 2010. http://archive.boston.com/news/local/massachusetts/articles/2010/02/28/no_picnic_for_teen_mothers.

"America's Sex Education: How We Are Failing Our Students." University of Southern California, Department of Nursing, September 18, 2017. https://nursing.usc.edu/blog/americas-sex-education.

Baker, Daizchane. "An Intimate Look at Life as a Teen Mom." *Teen Vogue*, January 27, 2014. https://www.teenvogue.com/story/teen-mom.

Body and Mind Staff. "Young Moms Hope to Break Cycle of Teen Pregnancy." *Penn Live*, August 23, 2009. https://www.pennlive.com/bodyandmind/index.ssf/2009/08/federal_grant_helps_state_coal.html.

Brady, Krissy. "13 Facts About Teen Pregnancy That Will Blow Your Mind." *Teen Vogue*, May 4, 2016. https://www.teenvogue.com/story/teen-pregnancy-prevention-facts.

Bruenig, Elizabeth. "Why Do Teen Girls in America Want to Get Pregnant?" *New Republic*, January 27, 2015. https://newrepublic.com/article/120856/american-teen-girls-have-more-pregnancies-fewer-abortions.

Burns, Janet. "Research Confirms That Abstinence-Only Education Hurts Kids." *Forbes*, August 23, 2017. https://www.forbes.com/sites/janetwburns/2017/08/23/research-confirms-the-obvious-that-abstinence-only-education-hurts-kids.

Carnwath, Ally, and Katie Toms. "It's Not Like Other Teenage Films. It Didn't Try to Make Pregnancy All Bad." *Guardian*, February 2, 2008. https://www.theguardian.com/film/2008/feb/03/features.review.

Carter, David. "Comprehensive Sex Education for Teens Is More Effective Than Abstinence." *American Journal of Nursing* 112, no. 3 (March 2012): 15. https://journals.lww.com/ajnonline/Fulltext/2012/03000/Comprehensive_Sex_Education_for_Teens_Is_More.5.aspx.

Chen, Joyce. "Solange Knowles Recalls Growing Up with Beyoncé and Being a Teen Mom." *Us Weekly*, February 9, 2017. https://www.usmagazine.com/celebrity-news/news/solange-recalls-growing-up-with-beyonce-being-a-teen-mom-w466113.

DoSomething.org. "11 Facts About Teen Pregnancy." Accessed on November 1, 2018. https://www.dosomething.org/us/facts/11-facts-about-teen-pregnancy.

Elder, Adam. "Three Different Teen Dads from Three Different Generations." *MEL*, May 4, 2017. https://melmagazine.com/en-us/story/three-different-teen-dads-from-three-different-generations.

Gann, Jen. "22 Women on What Breastfeeding Actually Feels Like." *The Cut*, March 23, 2017. https://www.thecut.com/2017/03/what-does-breastfeeding-feel-like.html.

Grady-Pawl, Spencer. "Linking Religion and Teen Pregnancy—There's a Map for That." *Humanist*, June 28, 2017. https://thehumanist.com/commentary/linking-religion-teen-pregnancy-theres-map.

Guttmacher Institute. "Sex and HIV Education." Last updated November 1, 2018. https://www.guttmacher.org/state-policy/explore/sex-and-hiv-education.

Hartmann, Lauren. "What Giving Birth Really Feels Like, According to 18 Moms." *Cosmopolitan*, November 13, 2015. https://www.cosmopolitan.com/sex-love/news/a49259/what-giving-birth-really-feels-like-according-to-18-moms.

Hartshorn, Jessica. "The 24 Hours After Giving Birth." *Parents*. Accessed on December 3, 2018. https://www.parents.com/pregnancy/my-body/postpartum/the-24-hours-after-giving-birth.

Johnson, David. "American Babies Are Less Likely to Survive Their First Year Than Babies in Other Rich Countries." *Time*, January 9, 2018. http://time.com/5090112/infant-mortality-rate-usa.

Jones, Oliver. "From the *People* Archives: Jay Thomas Opens Up About Reconnecting with the Son He Placed for Adoption." *People*, August 24, 2017. https://people.com/tv/jay-thomas-reconnecting-son-jt-harding.

Karnasiewicz, Sarah. "The Children They Gave Away," *Salon*, May 11, 2006. https://www.salon.com/2006/05/11/fessler_qa.

Knowles, Solange. "Solange Wrote the Most Powerful Letter to Her Teenage Self." *Teen Vogue*, May 17, 2017. https://www.teenvogue.com/story/solange-knowles-letter-to-teenage-self-cover-story-music-issue.

Mayo Clinic Staff. "Teens and Sex: Protecting Your Teen's Sexual Health." Mayo Clinic, August 3, 2017. https://www.mayoclinic.org/healthy-lifestyle/sexual-health/in-depth/teens-and-sex/art-20045927.

McFadden, Joyce. "What Happens to Our Girls When We Don't Talk About Sex." *Washington Post,* May 21, 2015. https://www.washingtonpost.com/news/parenting/wp/2015/05/21/what-happens-to-our-girls-when-we-dont-talk-about-sex.

Mulgrew, Kate. "Kate Mulgrew: The Child I Gave Up." *AARP The Magazine,* 2015. https://www.aarp.org/entertainment/style-trends/info-2015/celebrity-kate-mulgrew-adoption.html.

Nixon, Robin. "Adolescent Angst: 5 Facts About the Teen Brain." *Live Science,* July 8, 2012. https://www.livescience.com/21461-teen-brain-adolescence-facts.html.

O'Connell, Meaghan. "What Do Contractions Feel Like? 18 Women Respond." *The Cut,* March 26, 2015. https://www.thecut.com/2015/03/18-women-on-what-contractions-really-feel-like.html.

Office of Adolescent Health, US Department of Health and Human Services. "Breaking the Cycle of Intergenerational Teen Pregnancy Using a Trauma-Informed Approach." August 30, 2016. https://www.hhs.gov/ash/oah/sites/default/files/breakthecycle-traumainformed-slides.pdf.

———. "Trends in Teen Pregnancy and Childbearing." Last reviewed June 2, 2016. https://www.hhs.gov/ash/oah/

adolescent-development/reproductive-health-and-teen-pregnancy/teen-pregnancy-and-childbearing/trends/index.html.

Planned Parenthood. "Abortion." Accessed on November 1, 2018. https://www.plannedparenthood.org/learn/abortion.

———. "Parental Consent and Notification Laws." Updated June 2018. https://www.plannedparenthood.org/learn/teens/preventing-pregnancy-stds/parental-consent-and-notification-laws.

Power to Decide. "Survey Says: Support for Birth Control." January 2017. https://powertodecide.org/what-we-do/information/resource-library/survey-says-support-for-birth-control-january-2017.

RAND Corporation. "RAND Study Is First to Link Viewing of Sexual Content on Television to Subsequent Teen Pregnancy." November 3, 2008. https://www.rand.org/news/press/2008/11/03.html.

Reimer, Susan. "Think Only 'Their' Teens Get Pregnant?" *Baltimore Sun*, November 2, 2009. http://articles.baltimoresun.com/2009-11-02/news/0911010045_1_teen-pregnancy-teen-births-single-parent-families.

Rosenberg, Alyssa. "A Problematic TV Trend This Fall: Pregnant and Engaged Teenagers." *IndieWire*, October 10, 2013. https://www.indiewire.com/2013/10/a-problematic-tv-trend-this-fall-pregnant-and-engaged-teenagers-208148.

Silverman, Lauren. "In Texas, Abstinence-Only Programs May Contribute to Teen Pregnancies." NPR's *Morning Edition*, June 5, 2017. https://www.npr.org/sections/health-shots/2017/06/05/530922642/in-texas-abstinence-only-programs-may-contribute-to-teen-pregnancies.

Tobah, Yvonne Butler. "Could an Abortion Increase the Risk of Problems in a Subsequent Pregnancy?" Mayo Clinic, July 19, 2017. https://www.mayoclinic.org/healthy-lifestyle/getting-pregnant/expert-answers/abortion/faq-20058551.

Tourjée, Diana. "Trans Youth Get Pregnant at the Same Rate as Cisgender Peers." *Vice Broadly*, September 8, 2016. https://broadly.vice.com/en_us/article/mbqj5x/trans-youth-get-pregnant-at-the-same-rate-as-cisgender-peers.

Trenholm, Christopher, Barbara Devaney, Ken Fortson, Lisa Quay, Justin Wheeler, and Melissa Clark. *Impacts of Four Title V, Section 510 Abstinence Education Programs: Final Report*, Princeton, NJ: Mathematica Policy Research, 2007. https://aspe.hhs.gov/report/impacts-four-title-v-section-510-abstinence-education-programs.

Bibliography

WashingTeenHelp. "David's Story." Accessed on December 3, 2018. http://www.washingteenhelp.org/pregnancy/david-story.

"What Every Parent Should Know About Teen Pregnancy." HuffPost Contributor. Last updated June 1, 2015. https://www.huffpost.com/entry/what-every-parent-should-know-about-teen-pregnancy_b_6972590.

Wilson, Jacque. "Study: MTV's *16 and Pregnant* Led to Fewer Teen Births." CNN, January 13, 2014. https://www.cnn.com/2014/01/13/health/16-pregnant-teens-childbirth/index.html.

Wiltz, Teresa. "Racial and Ethnic Disparities Persist in Teen Pregnancy Rates." Stateline, The Pew Charitable Trusts, March 3, 2015. https://www.pewtrusts.org/en/research-and-analysis/blogs/stateline/2015/3/03/racial-and-ethnic-disparities-persist-in-teen-pregnancy-rates.

# Index

# About the Author

**Kristin Thiel** is a writer from Portland, Oregon. She has written numerous books on topics ranging from science and technology, to biographies, to history and current affairs. Thiel is the author of *Helping Yourself, Helping Others: Dealing with Eating Disorders.*